The Martian Tales

Marilee Robin Burton
Illustrated by Kristin Barr

Rigby®

A Harcourt Achieve Imprint

www.Rigby.com
1-800-531-5015

Literacy by Design Leveled Readers: *The Martian Tales*

ISBN-13: 978-1-4189-3918-2
ISBN-10:   1-4189-3918-8

Printed in China
1A 2 3 4 5 6 7 8 985 13 12 11 10 09 08 07

 # Contents

⇒✷ Chapter 1
Summer Begins

"Sanders, are you up?" his mother asked, knocking on his door.

Of course he was! It was the last day of school before summer. He and his best friend Joey had tons of summer plans. "Yes," he answered. Ready for the day, Sanders bounded downstairs happily.

Breakfast was strangely quiet that morning, but Sanders didn't think much about that. His mind was filled with thoughts about the day ahead.

Once at school, Sanders stood on a chair to take down the model of the solar system he and Joey had created. Sanders was going to take it home with him. He and Joey had been working together ever since Mrs. Ryan had asked them to be partners on a report on the planet Mars. They joked that their friendship had started on Mars.

Sanders hadn't expected to become best friends with Joey. After all, Sanders was a quiet kid. Joey was noisy and all over the place. They'd ended up being friends anyway.

Mrs. Ryan called the class together. She had a box full of gifts. "This has been a great year," Mrs. Ryan told them. "We've learned a lot. But learning doesn't stop when summer begins. I hope that you'll all write about your summer observations."

Mrs. Ryan handed Sanders the first package. Inside was a journal. Sanders thought it might be fun to write about the things he and Joey did together this summer.

"Remember, goodbye is just a beginning," Mrs. Ryan told her students as they walked out the door.

Sanders decided to walk home backward. "So I can look back on the year," he'd told Joey. Of course, walking backward also made him trip on a rock.

As Sanders picked himself up off the ground, Joey picked up the rock to examine it. "Looks lucky," he said. Joey had been collecting rocks forever.

"Lucky for who?" Sanders asked. "I tripped over it!"

"Lucky for us!" Joey said. "It's red like a Martian rock. It must mean it's going to be a good summer." He slipped the rock in his pocket.

The boys headed off in opposite directions. A few minutes later Sanders pushed his front door open.

"Anybody home?" he called as he headed into his room. He climbed up on a chair and hung the model from the light fixture so the solar system dangled above his desk. He was especially proud of how he and Joey had made sure Mars had its two moons.

Sanders could hear his parents talking in the kitchen. They sounded serious. Sanders headed over to them.

"What's up?" Sanders asked. He never expected that his world would soon turn upside down.

"Your mother and I have been having some trouble lately," his dad said. "We need some time alone. We're going to separate for a little while." His parents explained that they loved him very much and that he was the most important thing in both their lives.

Sanders wanted to say, "Can't you talk it out? You always tell me to talk it out when I have a problem." But the only words that came out were, "You can't!" He couldn't even ask the most important question: what would happen to him?

Sanders ran up to his room. He felt as though he needed to escape.

His heart was racing. His stomach was upset. He needed to be in his private tent. Sanders pulled his tent from under his bed and set it up in the middle of his bedroom. He grabbed his new journal and started to write.

MARS JOURNAL

Earth Date: June 22, 1:43:11 p.m.

My name is Sanders Parker and I'm from Mars. I was sent to Earth in a rocket ship. My mission is to convince my Earth parents to stay together and report back to Mars.

My parents have no knowledge of this. They believe I am their natural Earth child. I didn't even remember I was a Martian until today. When I came home from school, my parents told me they weren't getting along. They told me they were separating. That's when I remembered.

The Martians saw this coming and wanted to get the inside scoop on parent trouble from a kid's point of view. I wonder what my Martian parents are like. I bet they will never separate. Parents on Mars stay together.

Chapter 2
Relocation

Sanders tried to pretend things were normal. The next day he found some slugs from his mother's garden to relocate. When Sanders got to Joey's house with a bag full of slugs in his hand, Joey was outside waiting for him. Slug relocation was an idea that had come from Sanders' mother. She didn't want to poison the slugs, but she didn't want them eating her geraniums, either.

"How many?" Joey asked.

"Thirty-three," Sanders answered. He didn't mention his parents' separation to Joey. Saying anything out loud about it would make it more real. So he just asked, "Where do you think we should put them?"

Joey found several good bushes. They put
thirty of the slugs under five bushes, dividing
them into groups of six. They reserved three
slugs for scientific investigation, after which
they too would be relocated.

"Take the slugs to my room," Joey said.
"I'll go find something to keep them in."

Sanders walked into Joey's room. There was the Martian rock. "A lucky rock from Mars," Sanders said. He picked it up to study it more closely. It made him feel good to hold the Martian rock, like it belonged there in his hand.

Sanders knew that it was a plain old rock and that it was Joey's. But when he heard his friend's footsteps, it was as if his head forgot to tell his hands what to do. He stuffed the rock into his pocket before he could think about it.

"How's this for the slugs?" Joey asked, holding up a container.

"Perfect," Sanders said.

Sanders held Joey's rock all the way home. He wasn't sure why he'd taken it. He knew that it wasn't right to take things without asking—even a rock. He felt really bad to be sneaking something from a friend, especially Joey, his best friend.

"Sanders, come in here," his father called from the living room.

His parents were there. They sure were talking a lot for two people who wanted time apart.

"I just got off the phone with Grandpa," his mother said.

"Is he okay?" Sanders asked. He hadn't seen his grandpa since last summer, when the family had gone to Gram's funeral. He'd been close to Gram. Sanders didn't really know his grandpa at all.

"He's fine. He'd like you to stay with him this summer."

"What?" Sanders asked. Why would his grandfather want him to visit? Sanders needed to stay close to home. He had a mission. Why were his parents sending him away?

"Think about it," said his father. "Summer at your grandpa's would be fun."

"I don't want to go," Sanders said, his hand tightening around Joey's rock. How could he get his parents to change their minds about separating if he wasn't here with them?

"It would be good for Grandpa, too," his mother added. "He's been lonely since Gram died."

"I already have plans for the summer," Sanders said, his voice cracking.

"Sandy," his father said, "we can't always do what we want. You'll understand better when you're older. Your mother and I think it would be good for you to spend the summer with Grandpa. It will give us time to sort things out. And I'm not going to be here that much. I've accepted a transfer to a different office for the summer."

"I'm not going to be home much, either," his mother said. "I'll be working extra hours, and I need you to be taken care of."

"I'm old enough to take care of myself," Sanders protested.

"Honey, this isn't going to be easy for any of us," his mother said sadly. "But I know you'll have a good time."

Sanders' hand tightened around the rock. He couldn't give it back to Joey. Not yet.

✦

He had almost a week before he had to leave for Maine. It wasn't enough.

"Rough deal," Joey said. He was disappointed that they wouldn't be spending the summer together.

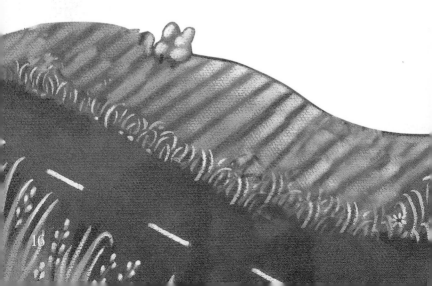

Sanders didn't tell him much about the separation. He didn't tell Joey about being from Mars at all, or about the rock he had taken from Joey.

★

Now Sanders sat inside his tent. Outside the tent lay his duffel bag, packed and waiting. The Mars rock wasn't packed. He would carry it in his pocket.

"I don't want to go," he'd told his father that morning, really meaning, "I don't want you to leave."

"I love you," his father had replied. Dad would be driving south at the same time that Sanders and his mother would be flying to Maine. They would be going in completely different directions.

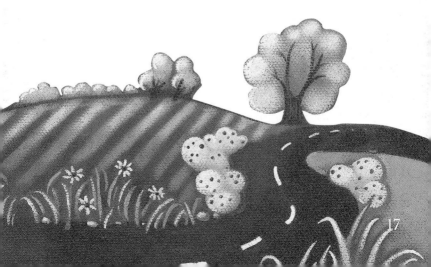

MARS JOURNAL

Earth Date: June 29, 9:05:10 A.M.

Everybody on Mars knows kids make the best plans and decisions. On Earth, parents are allowed to make all the decisions without ever asking kids what they want to do.

On Mars, kids get to make all the decisions, because kids are smarter than grown-ups.

On Mars, if parents need time alone, they go for a walk. They don't send kids away for the whole summer. I don't want to go to Maine. I want to go where I belong—to Mars.

It was afternoon when Sanders and his mother drove into the town of Shady Point. "Do I have to stay the whole summer?" he asked. He thought he'd ask one final time, just in case.

"I'm sorry, Sandy," his mother said. She turned down a dirt road. Sanders remembered the road from last summer, when they'd come to Gram's funeral. That had been sad. This was sad, too, in a different way.

They parked in front of the old wooden house. A tall man with white hair and a crooked nose walked from the porch to the car. "Good to see you," Grandpa said.

Sanders opened his door and slowly got out. What Sanders remembered most about his grandfather was his not saying much. He wondered what they would talk about this summer.

"Ready for summer in the country, Sanders?" his grandfather asked.

"Yes," Sanders said. What else could he say?

"Come inside and eat. Hot soup's good after a long trip," Grandpa said.

They all walked into the house.

When Sanders was done eating his soup, he wandered through the house. He walked into his grandfather's den and looked at the pictures. There was one of his mother and father, taken when they were much younger. Sanders was in the photo, too. His mother was holding him in her arms. Everyone looked happy.

Sanders decided to borrow the picture, just for a little while. He needed to remember that once he'd been in a happy family.

Chapter 3
A Martian in Maine

Sanders had been to Shady Point before, but last summer had been the summer of the funeral. They had only stayed for a few days.

The summer before that his grandmother had still been well. But Sanders hadn't visited Shady Point that year. Instead, Gram had visited San Diego without Grandpa. Sanders had taken her to the zoo while she was there.

Now Mom was gone and it was just Sanders and his grandfather. It was okay, Sanders guessed, but he figured they had already said everything they had to say to each other. He'd explored just about everywhere there was to explore. He didn't think there was that much more to see.

He already knew there were no solar systems dangling above his desk. No private tent in his bedroom. No parents.

MARS JOURNAL

Earth Date: July 5, 11:31:29 A.M.

Today my Earth mom went back to San Diego. She left me here in Shady Point. It might be hard to make friends since I'm the only Martian here.

On Mars, we like parents to stay together. That's why we have two moons. They keep each other company and remind parents to stay together. Parents on Mars don't send their kids away for the summer. Kids should stay with their parents. I told my Earth parents that. But they didn't understand.

Sanders wanted to find a private place to be alone. But he didn't want to ask where he could find a private place because then it wouldn't be private.

However, even without his own place, Sanders had lots of time alone. His grandfather seemed to see that he needed that time. Or maybe it was Grandpa who wanted to be alone. Every morning after breakfast, Grandpa would announce that he had "personal business" and go somewhere on his own—into his den or outside. Meanwhile, Sanders would explore or write in his journal.

It felt like it had been a hundred years since he had left San Diego.

MARS JOURNAL

Earth Date: July 8, 10:22:22 A.M.

Sometimes when you travel through space you have to go a really long way from home. If you travel from Mars to Earth, that's only 48,546,000 miles. But if you travel from Mars to Saturn, that's 743,442,000 miles. If you want to go from Mars to Pluto, that's 3,516,702,000 miles. And if your mother's on one planet, and your father's on another, and your best friend's on another . . . Do you have any idea how far away you feel from everyone?

The next morning they walked to downtown Shady Point. On the way a kid named Eric who lived next door to Grandpa said hello to them. Sanders had noticed him tossing a ball in the yard the day before.

"Hey, Mr. Roberts!" Eric said. He was being pulled along by a husky dog on a leash. "Slow down, Groucho!" he shouted, but the dog kept going. "Haven't seen you lately. That your grandson?"

"Yes. Eric. Sanders."

"Hi," said Sanders.

"He's trying to train the dog," Grandpa explained after Eric had been pulled away.

"He's not doing a very good job, is he?" Sanders asked.

"No. But some things take time."

The walk to town took time, too. Sanders had started kicking a rock on the path in front of him, a craggy gray rock that had caught his eye. He kicked it because he wanted to kick Shady Point. The rock was as close as he could come. So he kicked it again and again.

Sanders left the rock outside the post office. Grandpa wanted to buy stamps.

"Good to see you in town again!" said the gray-haired woman at the counter. "Sure don't see you around much anymore. Is this your grandson?"

"It is," Grandpa answered. "Dorothy, this is Sanders. Sanders, this is Mrs. Samuels."

"Hello," Sanders said.

"He looks a lot like you," Mrs. Samuels said. "He's kind of quiet like you, too, isn't he?"

"Maybe," said Grandpa.

"You know," Mrs. Samuels went on, "I think he has Margaret's eyes." Margaret was Sanders' grandma.

His grandfather looked at Sanders intently, nodded, and then looked away.

"So what can I do for you?" Mrs. Samuels asked.

"Any new stamps?" Grandpa asked.

"Just these," she said, laying some stamps on the counter. The first sheet showed African animals. The second had famous cowboys. The third showed stars and planets.

"Those," Sanders said, suddenly interested. He pointed to the third sheet.

Grandpa bought the stamps. They said goodbye and went back outside where Sanders retrieved his kicking rock. He didn't think he was like his grandfather at all. He dropped the kicking rock into his pocket next to the Martian rock.

"You interested in astronomy?" his grandfather asked.

"We learned about outer space this year," Sanders offered.

"Your grandmother liked to look at the stars. I bought her a handheld telescope for her birthday."

Sanders hadn't known that. "Do you still have the telescope?" he asked.

"I do," said Grandpa.

"Do you ever use it?"

"Not really," Grandpa said.

"Could I use it?" Sanders asked.

"Don't know," Grandpa said, smiling.

"Do you miss Gram very much?" Sanders asked. Suddenly he wondered about this more than he had even the summer before, when she had died.

"Yes, I surely do," Grandpa said.

Chapter 4
Stargazing

That evening, Sanders talked to his father. He said he missed Sanders and loved him. He even told Sanders that he had taken the solar system mobile with him so that he'd have something that reminded him of Sanders. But he didn't say that he was coming home soon or that Sanders could come home soon.

After the phone call, Sanders walked quietly back to his room.

"Sanders?" Grandpa knocked on the door of Sanders' room.

Sanders didn't answer.

"Can I come in?" Grandpa stuck his head inside the door. Sanders shrugged. Grandpa came inside and sat next to him. "Sad call?" he asked.

"I miss them. I want to go home. I want Dad to come home. I want to play with Joey," Sanders said.

"Hmmm," said Grandpa, nodding his head. He didn't tell Sanders not to be sad or that things would work out fine. Somehow Sanders knew that when Grandpa said "hmmm," he was really saying, "I know how you feel."

Sanders rolled the Martian rock around and around in his hand.

"Can I see?" Grandpa asked.

"Yeah," Sanders said, handing over the lucky rock, which hadn't been all that lucky yet.

Grandpa took the rock and examined it closely. "Nice rock," he said.

"Mars," Sanders said without even thinking. He was filled up with so many things that he couldn't keep it all inside himself anymore.

"Mars?" his grandfather repeated.

Sanders asked, "Do you ever feel like you're from another planet?"

"Yes," Grandpa said. "Lately it seems like I'm from another planet most days."

He didn't press Sanders or ask him to explain himself. They just sat there together quietly.

After a while, Grandpa said, "I think you can see Mars in the sky from here."

"You can?" asked Sanders.

"Yes. Especially with Gram's telescope."

They brought the flashlight and Gram's telescope. The telescope was made of brass and had a ring of purple at the eyepiece. Grandpa carried the telescope while Sanders held the flashlight, beaming it ahead of them so they could see the path. It was very dark at night in Shady Point, much darker than in San Diego. The only streetlights in Shady Point were downtown.

There seemed to be a lot more stars in Shady Point than in San Diego. But Grandpa said it was just that you could see more of the stars here.

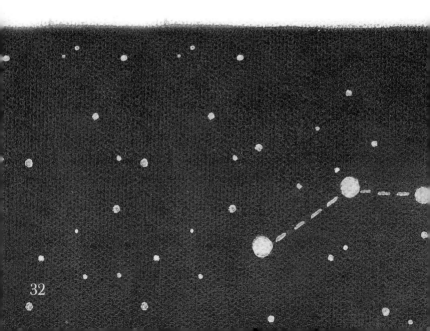

They walked over a little hill and past the graveyard where Sanders' grandmother was buried. They stopped at an open field. The sky looked like someone had poured a whole pitcher of sparkly stars into a big pot of black soup.

Sanders realized that he knew some of the constellations. "There's the Big Dipper," he said.

Grandpa showed Sanders how to find Mars. Sanders followed Grandpa's finger as it traced the path from the Big Dipper to Mars. They could both see Mars without even looking through the telescope.

Then Grandpa gave Sanders the telescope. Sanders used it to get a better look at Mars, but Grandpa took the telescope back again after a few minutes. "That's enough. Let's go back to the house."

The two of them walked back, Sanders holding the flashlight and Grandpa cradling Gram's telescope.

MARS JOURNAL

Earth Date: July 16, 10:20:11 P.M.

I've seen Mars every night this week. Grandpa and I go out, usually a little after sunset. That's the best time to see the planets. We've seen all the planets you can see without a telescope. I've seen Mercury, Venus, Mars, Jupiter, and Saturn.

Grandpa says it's good to be able to see things with your own eyes. He holds Gram's telescope while we look at the planets. Then he lets me use the telescope for a little while to look at the planets, but he never lets me have it for long.

When I talk to Dad, I tell him which planets Grandpa and I see. That way when he looks at the solar system mobile, he can think of me.

The next morning Sanders was surprised to see Eric standing by the falling-down fence separating his yard from Grandpa's yard.

"Hi! Aren't you Sanders?"

"Yeah," Sanders said. He was clutching a paper bag.

"What's in the bag?" Eric asked.

"Slugs," Sanders said.

"Can I see?" Eric asked. Sanders opened the bag and Eric peered inside. "What are you doing with them?"

"Relocating them," Sanders answered.

"Why?"

"I took them out of my grandpa's garden. They've been eating the lettuce. I figured I'd put them out back," Sanders said.

"Under the treehouse?" Eric asked.

"What treehouse?" Sanders asked.

"It was built a long time ago. I think your grandpa built it. Want to see it?" Eric said.

"Yeah," Sanders replied.

Eric climbed over the fence, and they walked to the back edge of the property. The treehouse was in the lower branches of a big tree. Its ladder was missing a lot of rungs. Sanders put the slugs in their new home at the foot of the tree. Then he and Eric carefully climbed up into the treehouse.

There was plenty of room for the two of them. "You're staying with your grandpa for the summer?" asked Eric.

"Yeah." It felt good to be talking to someone his own age. "I wanted to stay in San Diego, where my best friend is. But my parents wanted me to stay with my grandpa."

"I guess he could use some company," said Eric. "He mostly stays inside now. I was helping him fix that fence, but then he stopped working on it. My mom said he's changed since your grandma died. What do you do besides move slugs?"

"We've been looking at the planets with a telescope each night," Sanders answered.

"You have a telescope?" Eric said.

"It was my grandma's," Sanders explained.

"Do you think I could see her telescope?" Eric asked.

"I don't know," Sanders said. "Grandpa is pretty careful with it. I think it reminds him of Gram."

They hung out in the treehouse the rest of the afternoon. Sanders wondered if his mother had played in this treehouse. "It could probably be fixed," he thought. Then it could be his private summer place. Maybe he could even bring Gram's telescope and look at the stars with Eric.

After he and Eric said goodbye, Sanders decided to find Grandpa. He was probably in his den, seeing to his "personal business."

But Grandpa wasn't in his den. Sanders knew he was nearby, so he started looking around. Grandpa was just over the hill by the cemetery where Gram was buried. Grandpa was facing Gram's grave. His head was down, and he was talking too softly for Sanders to hear.

Sanders backed away. This was private time for Grandpa. He walked back to the house to wait for Grandpa to finish his personal business.

Chapter 5
The Treehouse

When Grandpa got back to the house, Sanders told him about finding the treehouse.

"I built that for your mother over thirty years ago," Grandpa said.

"Did she help you?" Sanders asked.

"Oh, yes," Grandpa said. "She was a very good helper."

Sanders wondered if his mother had liked helping her father. Now she lived so far away from Grandpa. Sanders wondered if she missed her father as much as Sanders missed his. "Grandpa," Sanders said slowly, "I saw you in the cemetery. Were you talking to Gram?"

His grandpa sighed. "I like to think that I am," he said. "Sometimes it feels good to pretend that she's listening."

"Sometimes I pretend stuff, too," Sanders whispered softly.

"Oh?" Grandpa said.

"I pretend I'm from Mars," Sanders said. "That it's my real home, because on Mars, parents don't separate."

"Hmmm," said Grandpa. It was the same "hmmm" as before. It said that Grandpa knew how Sanders felt.

"Grandpa," Sanders said, "do you think we can fix the treehouse?"

"Yes," said Grandpa. "I think we can."

MARS JOURNAL

Earth Date: July 18, 3:02:02 P.M.

I can *see* Mars with my naked eyes, but I can *see* it better with Gram's telescope. I can *see* the red places and the green places and maybe even the polar ice caps. Right near Mars is the star Spica. It is blue-white. From Earth, Spica and Mars look like they are close to each other, like they are friends. Lots of the stars look like they are close to each other, like friends and family should be.

They got ready to fix the treehouse early the next morning. Sanders helped his grandpa carry everything they needed for the repairs.

Grandpa filled the pockets of his tool belt with nails, a pencil, a hammer, and a tape measure. "I haven't worn this belt in a while," Grandpa said. "Guess I got out of the habit of fixing things."

At the treehouse, they started by pulling the rotting rungs off the tree. Then they

sawed a board into new rungs. Then they
hammered the new rungs to the tree. It was
hard work, but by lunchtime, the treehouse
ladder was fixed.

"Good job," said Grandpa. He was smiling
such a happy smile that Sanders smiled, too.

"Let's get some lunch," Grandpa said. "Hot
soup is good after hard work." They walked
back to the house.

MARS JOURNAL

Earth Time: July 20, 7:30:13 P.M.

Mars is much smaller than Earth. Like Shady Point is smaller than San Diego. Mars is a good planet, even if it's small, just like Shady Point is good, too. Shady Point doesn't have my parents or Joey, but it does have my grandpa and a clear night sky and a treehouse and Eric.

My mission was to stay in San Diego and explain to my parents why they had to stay together. But maybe it's not a Martian's job to tell people what to do, even if those people are your parents. They tell me they love me and that they're trying to work things out. Even if they split up, won't they still be my parents?

Chapter 6
The Telescope

Sanders had discovered that the treehouse made an even better private space than his tent back in San Diego. He could sit by himself, but at the same time he could see the world around him, the birds and animals and bugs. If he wanted to, he could have company, like Eric. There was plenty of room.

He wished he could take his grandmother's telescope up in the treehouse with him. That would make it perfect. Maybe if he borrowed the telescope and was really careful and brought it back in one piece, Grandpa would realize Sanders could be trusted with it.

So later that morning, Sanders took the telescope while his grandpa was out in the garden. Then he left, calling out to Grandpa, "I'm going to the treehouse for a while!"

"Okay," Grandpa said. "Come back for lunch."

When Sanders got to the treehouse, Eric was waiting for him. They climbed up into the treehouse together.

"You never said why your parents sent you here," Eric said. "Do you miss them?"

"Yeah," Sanders said. He hadn't told Eric about his parents yet. Sanders stared down at the floor. "They're having trouble," he finally said. "They're separated."

"Oh," Eric said knowingly. "My parents got divorced two years ago."

Sanders looked up in surprise. "Were you upset?"

"Yeah," Eric nodded. "But it's okay now. I don't see my dad every day, but I talk to him on the phone, and I spend vacations with him. I know he loves me. And my mom and I get along great." He was talking as though it were no big thing.

"They wanted to be alone this summer while they try to figure things out," Sanders told Eric.

"Things were bad when my parents first split up," said Eric. "They were both really sad. But it's better now."

"I guess it's hard for parents, too," Sanders said. He was feeling a little better. He reached into his backpack and carefully pulled out the telescope.

"Oh, cool!" said Eric. "Can I see?" He reached over and grabbed for the telescope. Sanders, startled, lost his grip. The telescope tumbled out of his hand and fell to the ground.

"I didn't mean to break it!" Eric said. "I'm sorry, Sanders."

They crouched under the treehouse. Sanders cradled the cracked and scratched telescope. Its lens was broken into pieces. Carefully Sanders picked up each fragment. "It's my fault," he finally said. "I wasn't supposed to take it." He wanted to blame Eric, but he knew he'd borrowed too many things. "I better go back. Grandpa's expecting me for lunch."

After lunch, Sanders didn't go back outside. Nor did he tell Grandpa about the telescope. Instead he headed up to his room.

"Not going to the treehouse?" Grandpa asked him.

"No," was all Sanders said.

Grandpa didn't ask any more questions, leaving Sanders alone. Grandpa never pushed Sanders to talk, but this time, Sanders wished he would. Then he could get the telling over with. But Grandpa didn't push, and Sanders wasn't brave enough to tell.

Sanders stared at the telescope and wondered how to fix it.

They didn't go stargazing for the rest of the week while Sanders tried to gather his courage. Each time Grandpa asked him if he wanted to go, Sanders said, "I don't feel like it tonight." He wasn't sure if he meant he didn't feel like stargazing or he didn't feel like telling the truth about the telescope.

By the fifth night, Sanders couldn't take it anymore. He went up to his room and collected some things. He took them into the kitchen, where his grandpa was sitting. Sanders sat down beside him. He set a picture down on the table, the one he had borrowed from his grandfather's den. Next to that he set Joey's red rock. He kept the telescope in his lap. "Grandpa," Sanders said. "I have something to tell you."

"What is it?" Grandpa asked.

"I kind of borrowed some things," Sanders said softly.

"Did you now," said Grandpa, picking up the picture. "I was wondering where this was. You borrowed it?"

"Yes," said Sanders. "I was going to give it back to you."

"Well, that is what borrowing means," said Grandpa. "Is this your Martian rock?"

"No," Sanders said. "It's my friend Joey's. I borrowed it, too."

"Does Joey know that you borrowed it?" Grandpa asked.

"No," Sanders said.

"I see," said Grandpa. "I'm sure you had a good reason for taking it, but don't you think you ought to ask before borrowing other people's things?"

"Yes," Sanders said miserably. He couldn't say anything else for a while. He and Grandpa sat in silence.

Finally Grandpa said, "Is there something more you wanted to tell me?"

"Yes," Sanders said. He took a deep breath. "I borrowed Gram's telescope." He gently placed the battered telescope on the table. "And I broke it."

✦

The next day was quiet. But it wasn't a shared quiet, like before. This felt like an angry quiet. Grandpa hardly talked to Sanders at breakfast. Toward the end of the meal, Grandpa cleared his throat and said, "Think it's about time to send Joey's rock back?"

Sanders nodded, miserable.

"I'll get you a box," Grandpa said.

Sanders carefully packed the rock in the box. Before he taped it shut, he realized he should send the rock he'd kicked to Joey as well. Then Joey would have a Shady Point rock. Maybe that would help make up for not having the Mars rock for most of the summer.

Sanders and Grandpa walked to town and mailed Joey's package. On the way back, Sanders said, "I can get a job. I'll work for as long as it takes to earn enough money to fix Gram's telescope."

"No," said Grandpa. "I'm not sure it can be fixed. Some things can't."

"Oh," said Sanders. He wished Grandpa would yell at him. Sanders didn't know what Grandpa was thinking, and he was too afraid to ask. So for the next couple of days, he avoided Grandpa, only seeing him at meal times. He spent the rest of the time at the treehouse or in his room.

Three nights after Sanders had told his grandpa what he'd done, there was a knock at the door to his room. "Is it all right if I come in?"

"Yeah," said Sanders, surprised.

His grandpa came inside, carrying a bag in one hand. He sat down next to Sanders. "I'd like to talk to you."

"I'm so sorry," Sanders said in a rush. "I won't ever borrow anything again without asking. I promise. Are you still mad at me?"

"I wasn't ever really mad at you," Grandpa said. "I was disappointed, but not mad. I've been thinking these past few days. I figured something out."

"What did you figure out?" Sanders felt half relieved and half curious.

"Holding on to things doesn't bring people back, Sanders. It just makes you miss what's right in front of you. I loved your grandma so much I didn't want to lose any part of her. But I have something of hers that's far more important than a telescope. I have a grandson who has her eyes. Your grandma is gone now, but I still have a family." Grandpa smiled. "You helped me figure that out, Sanders."

Sanders didn't know what to say.

"I have something for you, Sanders," Grandpa continued. "It's something your grandma would have wanted you to have, so it's a gift from the both of us, because we love you." Grandpa reached into the bag and pulled out a package wrapped in starry paper. He handed it to Sanders.

Sanders carefully pulled off the wrapping paper. Inside was a brass telescope with a purple band. "You fixed Gram's telescope?" he whispered.

"Not exactly," said Grandpa. "Someone else put a new lens in. But I did knock out some of the dents."

Sanders stared down at the telescope. He could still see some scratches and dents. "Gram's telescope," he said in wonder.

"No, *your* telescope," Grandpa said. "You don't have to borrow it, because it belongs to you."

Sanders leaned over and hugged his grandpa. His grandpa hugged him back. "When you leave," Grandpa said, "I won't have a telescope anymore. So I was thinking that I'd visit you in San Diego. That way I can borrow the telescope when we go stargazing at night."

"That sounds wonderful," Sanders said.

MARS JOURNAL

Earth Date: August 8, 12:34:56 P.M.

My name is Sanders Parker and I am from Earth. I have a mother and father and grandpa and two best friends.

You can see a lot of stars at night. In the daytime, you don't see the stars because the sun shines so brightly. But the stars are still there. Even when they're not right there with you, your family is still your family. They're still there, just like the stars.